MW01255815

SLICE-FREE GOLF
In Three Easy Steps

More Power – No Banana Balls!

By Brian A. Crowell, PGA

With Foreword By Gary Player

Photography & Design
by Dave Donelson

SLICE-FREE GOLF
In Three Easy Steps

More Power - No Banana Balls!

By Brian A. Crowell, PGA

Photography & Design
by Dave Donelson

Published and printed in the United States of America
by Donelson SDA, Inc.

FIRST EDITION

ISBN: 978-1461199557

**Custom editions of *Slice-Free Golf* are available for
special promotions, premiums, and training.
For more information, contact brian@slicefreegolf.com.**

"My friend Brian Crowell can help you to get the most out of your swing. Slice-Free Golf is proof of both his effectiveness as a teacher and Brian's hatred of the dreaded slice."

-- **Gary Player**, winner of 18 major championships around the world

"If you slice, *Slice-Free Golf* is a MUST read...well-written, with humor!"

-- **Scott McCarron**, three-time winner on the PGA TOUR

"I've played in pro-ams for nearly 25 years...By far, the most frustrated and miserable golfers were the slicers. Follow Brian's lead and leave your slice in the kitchen. Golf can be powerful, satisfying and fun for everyone...cool book!!!"

-- **Dottie Pepper**, winner of 17 LPGA Tour events, including two major championships, Golf Commentator for NBC and The Golf Channel

"A book dedicated solely to curing the slice...and it works! *Slice-Free Golf* is truly one of a kind!"

-- **Rob Labritz**, PGA, 2009 Metropolitan PGA Player of the Year and Low Club Pro, 2010 PGA Championship

"Brian has done a masterful job! By providing you with 25 keys for getting rid of the banana ball, he has provided you with an opportunity for better golf!"

-- **Shawn Humphries**, PGA, Golf Magazine Top 100 Teacher

"Brian can help you with more than just your slice...you've gotta try *Slice-Free Golf*!"

-- **Debbie Doniger**, LPGA, Golf Digest Top 20 Under 40, Golf for Women Top 50 Instructor, ACC Hall of Fame

Table of Contents

More *Slice-Free Golf*

Dedicated to those who want to produce

more power with less effort.

Foreword
By Gary Player

Golf is a truly remarkable game that demands honesty, integrity and sportsmanship like no other. It brings people together to enjoy the spirit of competition and the beauty of our environment. No other sport can unite people of all ages and skill levels on the same field of play. If you take good care of your body, golf can be played for a lifetime.

I have had the good fortune to play golf competitively across the globe for almost 60 years, and with 18 major championships and winning The Career Grand Slam on both the PGA Tour and Champions Tour, I have certainly enjoyed success at golf's highest level. Trophies do not come easy, and my success required mental preparation, physical fitness, determination, practice and a positive attitude. In addition to my dedication and hard work, there was (and still is) another "weapon" that has served me well throughout my career: the draw.

The draw is a wonderful skill to possess. When you draw the ball, you hit it farther and more importantly, you can shape your shots. Learning to draw the ball is essential to lowering you score and getting the most out of your swing.

My friend Brian Crowell can help you to get the most out of your swing. I first met Brian in New York at a course I designed named GlenArbor Golf Club in 2006. He is an accomplished PGA instructor who has a very clear and comfortable way of communicating with his students. *Slice-Free Golf* is proof of both his effectiveness as a teacher and Brian's hatred of the dreaded slice.

Slice-Free Golf offers a clear step-by-step program for turning your slice into a draw. Brian offers 25 drills for slice-free golf, recommendations for training aids, and easy-to-understand full-color photography. Although this book is devoted entirely to eliminating the "banana ball", there are significant additional benefits. By following Brian's program, you will also develop more consistency, greater distance off the tee, and more enjoyment on the golf course.

Golf has been wonderful to me. I've enjoyed the victories...but this sport has also taken me to so many beautiful places, introduced me to so many special friends, and enabled me to make a difference in the world.

Don't let the slice diminish your enjoyment of this great game. If cutting the ball is frustrating you, please read *Slice-Free Golf*. Your score will improve and you'll have more fun on the links. Stay healthy & have fun with golf!

Best Wishes,

Gary Player

A Word About This Book

My reason for writing this book is simple. I was once the embarrassed owner of a hideous slice. I HATED it! In fact, the slice nearly drove me away from golf. But I hung in there long enough to find the simple keys to hitting a solid draw. I still remember the overwhelming joy and power I felt after connecting with my first *Slice-Free Golf* shot.

During my 20 years as a golf instructor it became painfully obvious that my struggle with the "banana ball" was not an isolated incident. I was not alone. Slicing is BY FAR the most prevalent challenge to the typical golfer. And believe it or not, slicing mechanics are the foundation for other top concerns such as inconsistency, trouble playing from the rough, and a lack of distance. After giving thousands of lessons, I found it abundantly clear that providing a simple, no-miss program to eliminate the slice would bring joy and happiness to golfers everywhere! Thus, the creation of *Slice-Free Golf*.

I've been teaching golf since 1991 and I'm currently the PGA Head Golf Professional at GlenArbor Golf Club in Bedford Hills, New York. In addition to my club pro duties, I host a radio show and can be seen on network television and the web as a golf analyst / commentator. I've covered dozens of major championships from all the professional tours. Suffice it to say, I have seen more than my share of golf swings, both good and not so good. Styles vary, even among the best players, but there are undeniable common denominators that exist in the most successful swings.

Slice-Free Golf will unveil those keys, outline a simple step-by-step program, and even supply you with dozens of slice-killing drills! To summarize, *Slice-Free Golf* changed my golfing life, and now it will change yours. Prepare to hit shots that you wouldn't have thought possible, and get ready to have more FUN!

After all, enjoyment of the game is the ultimate goal. Golf should make you laugh and even lighten your spirits. It can be a great escape from the serious issues we face all too frequently. I hope that readers will pick up that attitude from the way this book is written and see that improving your golf game doesn't have to be a stern, arduous business. Improvement can be an enjoyable journey. If I've done my job, not only will you get a chuckle from time to time, you will reap the benefits of a far more enjoyable golf game as you bid farewell to that evil, ugly slice.

-- Brian A. Crowell, PGA

Introduction To *Slice-Free Golf*

The slice haunts millions of golfers worldwide. After thousands of hours on the lesson tee during my 20 years as a golf instructor, two things remain extremely clear:

1. Golfers LOVE extra distance
2. Golfers HATE to slice

I guarantee that *Slice-Free Golf* will conquer BOTH issues and, perhaps more importantly, jump start your enthusiasm for the game of golf.

I'm sure you've asked yourself, why does it look so easy for the men and women pros on television? With this book, you will now be introduced to the same exciting and powerful style of golf that the best players in the world display, a style that actually requires far less effort than your current swing.

In three quick steps, *Slice-Free Golf* will eliminate your slice and add distance and consistency to your game. And if you follow the steps diligently, the transformation from slicer to long-baller will happen FAST!

Contrary to what you have probably experienced, drastically improving your golf swing does NOT need to be a long and challenging process.

What causes a slice?

The slice occurs when a golf club strikes a ball with a glancing blow that creates side spin. Energy in the form of the club head is moving on a path to the left of where the face of that club head is aiming prior to (and through) the moment of impact. The result is a golf ball that takes flight then spins off weakly to the right.

Although many golfers have learned to accept and make allowances for a slice, the shot severely limits the player's ability to play certain holes especially those that bend sharply to the left. The slice also robs a player of valuable distance—it is the WEAKEST shot in golf! A struggling golfer who announces, "I like to hit a fade" is most likely deluding himself because he is incapable of producing solid impact that leads to a straight shot or a draw (a shot that curves gently from right to left). Learn how to eliminate the slice once and for all and you will pick up a massive increase in distance!

Some slice facts

- Approximately 82% of all golfers regularly slice.
- Only 18% of all golfers produce a consistent draw.
- The average USGA handicap of those who draw the ball is 15 strokes lower than that of those who slice.
- Eliminating the slice can be the fastest way to lower your scores.
- A draw-swing produces distances up to 30% GREATER than a slice-swing using the same amount of effort.
- A ball driven with slice spin flies weakly with less forward energy and lands softly with minimal forward roll...
- A ball driven with draw spin flies farther and is more likely to roll forward after landing.
- Golfers who struggle to drive a ball 200 yards can pick up an additional 50 YARDS with *Slice-Free Golf!*

Why is the *Slice-Free Golf* method better?

- Retain your own individual style

All successful swings DO NOT look alike. The World Golf Hall of Fame is filled with varying styles—slow and loose, fast and compact, upright, flat, one-plane, two-plane, weight shifters, stack and tilters, etc. There are many ways to get the job done. Although *Slice-Free Golf* asks you to adhere to a three-step process, it also allows for a variety of swing characteristics.

- Easy to follow program

Slice-Free Golf shows you how to harness all of your energy and channel it into the proper path, so that you gather every single yard of distance possible. *Slice-Free Golf* maps out your journey to powerful, slice-free distance in three simple steps accompanied by unique instructional photos.

- Fast results

Just follow the steps. Extra distance and solid contact through the elimination of your slice will happen FAST so there is no need to wait patiently. You will notice the difference on your very next trip to the tee!

- Total dedication

There are countless golf instruction books on the market, but none of them are so clearly focused on one specific goal: SLICE ELIMINATION. The sole objective of *Slice-Free Golf* is to unveil the secret of a pure, draw-producing swing. Every reader who follows the three steps in this book will experience powerful, solid contact.

- Permanent change

Slice-Free Golf is NOT a band-aid or a quick fix. This method is easy to understand, and it is easy to implement, but the transformation from slicer to long-ball hitter is PERMANENT. You will enjoy the sweet feel of producing a draw for the rest of your life!

- 100% Proven Success

I have fine-tuned the three steps to *Slice-Free Golf* throughout my 20 years as a golf instructor. Prior to entering the golf business, I was a slicer myself. Using the same principles that you are about to learn, I rapidly transformed my weak, fading shots into powerful distance. My scores dropped from the low 90s to the low 70s in less than six weeks. While you may not drop 20 strokes before the end of this season, I can promise you dramatic improvement FAST. Using the *Slice-Free Golf* program, I have NEVER failed to show a slicer the joy of a solid draw-producing swing. *Slice-Free Golf* is PGA Pro-tested and proven through thousands of hours of my research. You WILL feel the joy of *Slice-Free Golf!*

- Accompanying Support

For even more help—and a few entertaining tidbits—please visit www.slicefreegolf.com. You'll find a collection of swing tips, drills, videos, training aids, and other helpful items in addition to a blog where you can ask questions and make your own observations about *Slice-Free Golf*. You can also print handy pocket-size versions of the Bonus Drills in this book. Take them to the range or even to the course for a quick reminder.

Enjoy this experience! Follow the three steps to *Slice-Free Golf* and I promise you will see exciting game-changing results the very next time you step on the tee. *Slice-Free Golf*...there is NO better way to play this great game!

A sincere apology to left-handed readers

My sister is left-handed, I have close friends who are left-handed, Phil Mickelson plays golf left-handed. They all are wonderful people whom I respect and admire. However, in order to keep my instruction as simple as possible, I will be writing this book from a right-handed point-of-view. I mean no disrespect to the southpaws, but the vast majority of people play golf from the other side of the ball.

Please keep this fact in mind as you continue with *Slice-Free Golf*. Many lefties are familiar with transposing golf advice, and the beautiful photos throughout this book will certainly clarify the proper perspective. While every word of advice on the following pages is as pertinent to lefties as it is to righties, the lefties will need to flip directions and images (or look at the pictures in a mirror...I'm not kidding...try it). If you're new to instruction and you're left-handed, please note this important distinction.

Your commitment

Changing habits is rarely easy, especially when you've done something the same way for an extended period of time. But if you love golf (or *want* to love golf) and you are a slicer, you NEED to change! A life without slicing is a life you must experience. Once you turn to *Slice-Free Golf*, there is no turning back. You will feel the crisp, sweet and explosive contact associated with a draw, the most pleasing of flights where the ball leaves the clubface on a path slightly right of the target line and works its way back to the left to land on-target. You will wonder how you ever made it this far in golf with a weak, disgusting slice.

And although I solemnly vow to lead you proudly to the promised land of the no-banana balls, you must first make a serious commitment to give *Slice-Free Golf* your undivided attention. If you pledge to follow this book step-by-step, your slice will evaporate and your enjoyment of golf will increase dramatically. However, if you think you know most of this stuff already and just want to try a step or two without putting the time and effort into the complete *Slice-Free Golf* sequence, then ALL BETS ARE OFF! In fact, without serious commitment, you are likely to wallow forever in the wimpy world of slicing.

If you cannot commit to trying the simple three-step *Slice-Free Golf* program, you have my sincere condolences. Please give this book to one of your slicing buddies, then go find an ATM and make a sizable withdrawal. You will need the cash to pay off losses to your friends as they continue to kick your wimpy, slicing ass on the golf course for years to come. So what's it gonna be?!?!

DRAW	or	**SLICE**
STRENGTH	or	**WEAKNESS**
POWER	or	**POWDER PUFF**
CONFIDENCE	or	**INDECISION**
PRIDE	or	**EMBARRASSMENT**
GOOD	or	**EVIL**

All right, maybe I'm taking this a bit too far, but you get the idea. Commit to giving *Slice-Free Golf* your total attention. True change requires determination, but you will be rewarded handsomely. Let's start!

Step One

•

Get Set

Get Set Key #1

Align Your Base

I know what you're thinking… Oh, great! Yet another instruction book wasting my time talking about alignment. But trust me, this won't take long, and it's not a waste of time because it's a critical step in the *Slice-Free Golf* system.

There are many alignment points that can be evaluated, but for the sake of simplicity, I have narrowed them down to just two separate components, your base and your upper body. Get Set Key #1 addresses the alignment subject you have heard the most about, your feet. Actually it requires identifying the target line and becoming very aware of the position of feet, knees, and hips as they relate to this line. I wrap this all into the category of Base Alignment, which is the first of the two alignment components. The second will be covered in Get Set Key #3.

The first thing to do is to figure out where you want the ball to go when you hit it. Don't laugh! Determining the true target line is not something you should take lightly since the effectiveness of every step to come is based on this being done carefully.

Take an extra minute to lay down guides that are perfectly parallel to your chosen target line as a reference. One should be just outside where the ball lies, the other where your feet will be.

Now take your stance and look at your feet relative to the closest guide.

Slicers align their feet in a variety of ways, but believe it or not, the closed position is very common.

An open base alignment occurs quite often as well.

After confirming your target line, we can now get your feet in the proper position. Like the guides you laid down, the proper position is parallel to the target line.

Although it's a bit trickier to see and assess, the heel line is a more accurate measure of foot alignment than the toe line.

This is because, depending on personal style and preference (and often due to range-of-motion issues) the toe of either shoe might be flared out...

(or even toed in), which can affect your perception of true alignment.

Although there are always some allowances for style, make sure there isn't excessive flare, and get your heels parallel to that target line.

When your feet are aligned parallel to the target line, chances are pretty good that your knees and hips will follow suit—and if they haven't, make sure they do before you go any further. It might be helpful to have a friend stand behind you looking directly down the target line so they can check your alignment.

Once your feet, knees, and hips are square and aligned properly, you have successfully mastered Get Set Key #1 and your base is squarely aligned to the target.

Congratulations! Now proceed to Get Set Key #2.

Get Set Key #2

Ball Position

Now that your base alignment is square, solid and parallel to the target line, let's look at your ball position. Each *Slice-Free Golf* step is relatively simple yet each is critical for success. Physically, this one could be the simplest of them all, yet it is perhaps rather challenging mentally.

The reason proper ball position can be difficult for the slicer is that many of them feel if they position the ball forward (closer to the target) in their stance, they'll have more time to return the club face to a square or even closed position at impact, which would decrease their chances of producing a hideous slice. Ironically, what they are trying to avoid is even more likely to happen!

For the purposes of this chapter, I will assume you're setting up to hit a driver. You have probably heard that you should tee the ball even with your left instep when hitting driver.

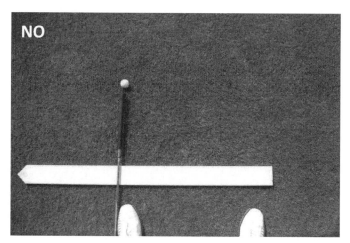

As I mentioned earlier, many chronic slicers tend to position the ball even further forward than that!

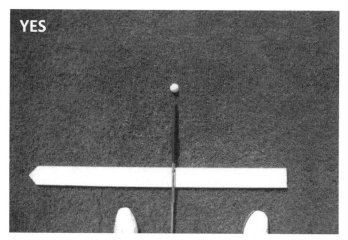

To officially complete Get Set Key #2, though, your ball position needs to come closer to the center of your stance. In fact, just one or two inches left of dead center is fine! Yes...for the driver!

I know that this new ball position is NOT going to look or feel good to you. Slicers normally feel like the ball is now waaay too far back, and they are certain that a ball struck from this position will launch too far to the right of the target line, but TRUST ME. You are now one step closer to a powerful draw!

It would be tempting to jump ahead and discuss the impact of a forward position on the transfer of energy from club to ball but, for the sake of simplicity, let's stay on task and take care of Get Set Key #2. I'll explain more later, but your golf ball needs to be further back (in some cases *much* further back) in your stance than you are accustomed to. This is true for all your clubs proportionally.

Congratulations! You've now mastered Get Set Key #2.

Get Set Key #3

Align Your Upper Body

Okay, with Get Set Keys #1 and #2 now under control, it's time to address the second component of alignment I alluded to earlier. Yes, proper pre-swing alignment is so crucial that I have dedicated TWO separate keys to it! Get Set Key #3 deals primarily with shoulder alignment. Once you get that right, good chest and forearm positions should follow suit.

Since he despises the thought of a ball being sprayed to the right, the typical slicer will settle into the address position with his shoulders aligned to the left .

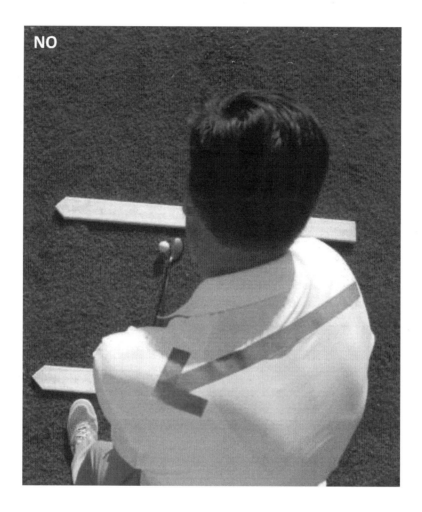

Now I don't blame the slicer for setting up this way. From this position, he feels confident that the ball will not be lost to the right. In fact, it *is* very likely that the ball will start left of the target line and slice back towards the center, which will keep the ball in play. It won't go as far as you want, but the ball will—hopefully—at least end up in the fairway.

But is that the way you want to play this game? NO! You want to ERADICATE YOUR SLICE!

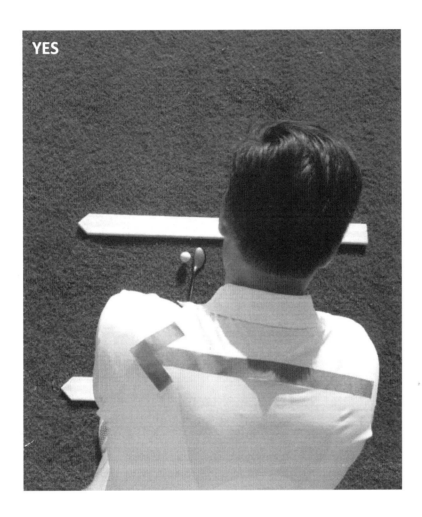

So now you must suck it up, raise the bar, and embrace the principles of *Slice-Free Golf!* It is likely to feel a little funky at first, but Get Set Key #3 requires you to position your shoulders not just for a straight shot , but for a draw. Yes, I'm asking that you aim your shoulder line a bit to the right of square.

From this view, you'll notice that my head and face stay in alignment with my shoulders. With a proper *Slice-Free Golf* set up, you will be looking slightly *behind* the ball.

These subtle but important changes will assist in creating draw spin. In fact if you think about it, the new ball position that you learned in Get Set Key #2 actually helps you to achieve the proper *Slice-Free Golf* upper body alignment. With the ball farther back in your stance, closing your shoulders makes total sense. You'll also notice that your left forearm is a touch higher (or farther from your belt buckle) than your right...perfect!

You may have noticed that I have not mentioned your grip or your club face yet. At this point, if you have achieved the proper positions outlined in Get Set Keys #1, #2, and #3, I am very proud of you. It is now time to address the club that is probably positioned INCORRECTLY in your hands.

DROP THE CLUB!

And read Get Set Keys #4 and #5 very carefully before you pick it up again.

Get Set Key #4

Square Your Clubface

This may seem obvious, but I'm going to say it anyway: The position of your clubface at impact is paramount to success. Having a solid clubface position at address leads to a better chance of proper position at impact.

Many slicers have slowly developed a closed clubface at address, meaning that the leading edge of the club is aimed to the left of the target line. This obviously makes sense to the slicer because a closed face is more likely to keep the ball from launching to the right (a slicer's fear). But a closed face is NOT the answer.

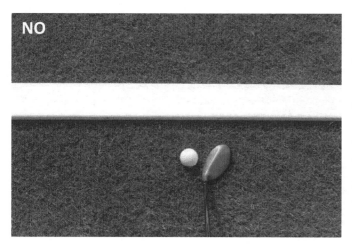

This photo shows the open position, where the leading edge is aimed to the right of the target line. This is the address position that is most likely to lead to a slice, but trust me, an ugly slice can be created from all three pictured positions.

It is important at this point in your *Slice-Free Golf* journey, for you to fully understand what a square clubface looks like at address. This square position is the objective of Get Set Key #4.

Before we move on, let's make sure the ball is TRULY in the center of the clubface. This can be tricky to determine from the address position. Due to your angle of view, a bit of an optical illusion is created. To get the proper perspective, look from directly over the ball (a bird's eye view) to make sure it is centered. Otherwise, what you see is NOT what you get.

What you see at address

Where the ball really is

What you *should* see

The ball is centered

Note that a ball that is truly centered may appear to be toward the toe of the club when you look from the standard address position, so be careful! The majority of slicers make contact toward the heel of the club and many banana bombers actually address the ball toward the heel (thinking it is centered). A ball that looks centered but is actually lined up toward the heel, is *much* more likely to be struck toward the heel at impact. And the most common trajectory resulting from heel contact? You guessed it—a lousy SLICE!

So in addition to clubface position, take a quick look from directly over the ball to make sure the ball is centered on the face as well.

One last check before you swing away. Find a leaf, dark spot, or other mark on the ground a few inches in front of the club face and directly on the target line. It will make a great—and legal— alignment aid on the course.

Now that you are armed with your new and improved *Slice-Free Golf* power draw set-up (Get Set Keys #1, #2, #3, and #4), ball position and clubface and their relationship to the target line are probably going to look much different. It is quite possible that these new positions will not fit your eye immediately. In fact, things may look downright weird! But you MUST TRUST the system. Remember that what *was* comfortable to your eye led to big, ugly slices.

In order to succeed with *Slice-Free Golf,* CHANGE is required!

All square?

Now that we know that the clubface is in the proper position,
it's time to officially take our grip!

Let's move on to Get Set Key #5.

Get Set Key #5

Your Grip

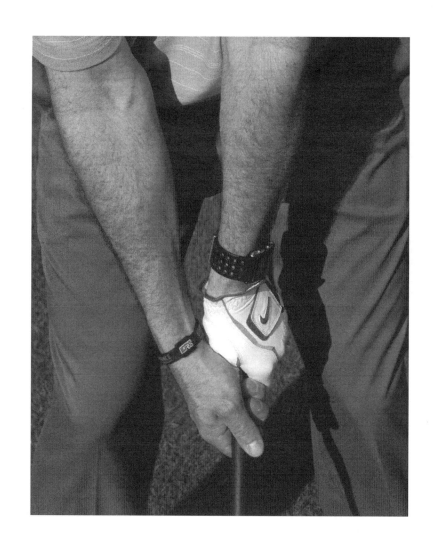

The grip is *very* personal. As a PGA instructor, I know how attached (literally) golfers are to the grip they've been using. After all, this is the only point where you actually make contact with the club. Let's face it, if some other part of your body is touching the club, you have bigger issues than slicing to address!

Which particular grip you use is not that important to me (although if you press me for my favorite, I would recommend the overlap), but the *position* of that grip on the club is VERY CRUCIAL!

How your grip relates to the clubface and the target line are of the utmost importance. Since your alignment and clubface are now good, it's time to learn the final pre-swing key in the *Slice-Free Golf* system, the grip.

Remember, this is the #5 Get Set Key (not #1) for a reason— your body from your feet to your head needs to be properly aligned, the ball in the right place, and the club face square to the target line BEFORE you grip the club!

A great way to start is to take a look at the butt end of your grip and imagine a clock face on it with 12 o'clock in line with a square leading edge.

Your thumb should NOT be centered on the twelve o'clock line (straight down the top of the grip).

Your left thumb needs to be centered on an imaginary line drawn at the one o'clock position.

It MUST be on that one o'clock line, which you will notice works perfectly with your new shoulder and forearm alignment.

As I said earlier, this may not be a new grip but it will seem different because it is likely to be a in a new position relative to the clubface and target line. From your vantage point at address, you should see two knuckles on your left hand, and two fingernails from your right middle and ring fingers.

I would recommend taking your time and actually practice taking this grip. Position the clubface properly (square to the target line) and begin by applying the left hand only .

Then carefully direct the right hand into position.

This new grip position will likely feel a bit strange, and certainly be a bit under the shaft compared to your previous position, but STICK WITH IT! It is important to trust this new grip orientation.

It is also very important to keep your hands relatively relaxed. Many slicers grip the club too tightly, or with varying degrees of tension. Your grip pressure should be consistent yet comfortable with supple wrists. Relaxed wrists lead to relaxed forearms, relaxed shoulders, etc., which in turn lead to a consistent, smooth and natural release during your swing.

Congratulations on completing Get Set Keys #1-#5. These keys comprise the pre-swing step, and each one is crucial for *Slice-Free Golf* success. Believe it or not, these first five keys are the most difficult to complete successfully. But once they're in place, you are prepared for the pure joy of solid contact and extra distance.

The dynamic (or swing) steps on the following pages are going to be very easy to follow. Many instructional materials have been made confusing and even contradictory by gurus and numerous media sources. But *Slice-Free Golf* will provide simple illustrated keys that will guide you to success—with plenty of room for your own individual style.

So FEAR NOT, the swing is truly the easy part.

Let's get started…

Step Two

•

Swing

Swing Key #1

Centered Turn

Step One has you ready for success. Now you need to focus on making a centered turn, which for many slicers will be an entirely new sensation.

Many slicers sway back (often rather severely) during the take-away

While others do the opposite and lean forward. BOTH can lead to an ugly slice.

Centered is what we're looking for!

Before moving on, I want to explain why staying centered is so vital to your success. A golfer who sways away from the target and is too far behind the ball at impact is destined to create a swing path that is commonly referred to as over-the-top or outside-in. This poor position can also be achieved by a golfer who first creates a reverse pivot by leaning forward during the backswing, then darting backward during the downswing.

In both cases, the path of the club head will clearly be moving significantly to the left of the target line prior to impact, leading to either a straight pull that will miss left of the target, a pull draw or hook that will miss even further to the left, or a hideous pull fade or slice that will start left and spin back weakly toward the target.

Losing centeredness in the other direction can be damaging as well. Having the center of the swing move toward the ball before or at impact can lead to an even steeper and more dramatic swipe across the ball.

The bottom line: make a centered turn!

Thanks to successfully completing Step One, you are already positioned perfectly. You simply need to make a full centered turn from that position. Of course "full" is a relative term. Depending on body type and flexibility, fullness will vary significantly from person to person. But I want you to think of a full turn in this way: turn as completely as you can while maintaining your height at address and keeping your axis (spine) centered. If you feel rising or any type of lateral movement, you may be over-turning—and there is no need for that.

Conversely, if you're barely taking the club back because you feel the farther back you go, the greater your chance of a miss-hit, suck it up and make as full a centered turn as you can.

In the photos for this step, you'll notice my left arm looks L-O-N-G, indicating excellent extension.

Now keep in mind that I'm fairly flexible, and this position is not all that easy to achieve, but that's okay! Even if your backswing is limited, and your left arm isn't *perfectly* straight, the important thing regarding the left arm is to keep it *relatively* long. It should NOT be STIFF and LOCKED, just relaxed and relatively long. Stretching and repetition can improve your range of motion, but it is more important to have a long, relaxed left arm than one that is STRAIGHT (which implies stiff and locked) and TIGHT. When you throw a ball, is your throwing arm tense and stiff or is it relaxed? That's right—it's relaxed. If you want to create speed, that arm is NOT tense! It is imperative that you maintain the feeling of left arm relaxation and extension as you move through the swing steps. Believe me, it will pay off!

At this point, with your centered turn and a relaxed and relatively long left arm, the club should be somewhere behind you as you prepare for the downswing, the subject of Swing Key #2.

Swing Key #2

Swinging Under the Foam

The steps you have completed to this point have now positioned you for a perfect downswing that travels under the foam. What in the world do I mean by "under the foam?"

Well, imagine you are addressing the ball, and just outside the ball stands a 4' x 8' sheet of two-inch thick Styrofoam insulation.

After cutting a hole in the foam for your head to fit through, the sheet is lowered down until it rests on your shoulders.

The legendary Ben Hogan famously used illustrations with a sheet of glass in much the same way (but trust me, it is *much* easier to work with the foam).

The centered turn from your new *Slice-Free Golf* address will position your club at the top of the swing without touching the imaginary foam board.

The challenge now is to remain centered and return the club to the ball *without endangering the foam*. Without successfully mastering the previous keys, this under-the- foam downswing is nearly impossible. But since you are diligently reading through each step, you are currently poised for glory!

We are at a pivotal moment in the swing, so I need you to pay VERY CLOSE ATTENTION! Swing Key #2 (and the imaginary foam board) will show you the power of proper swing path. Many slicers can manage to find the position shown in the previous photo, but as they begin the downswing, their shoulders rotate dramatically left (in an effort to keep the ball from starting to the right) and the club is thrown "over-the-top" through the imaginary foam board. This leads directly to energy (and divots) going left and balls slicing like mad.

The foam board idea enforces what we intuitively understand: the club, on an efficient path from the top of the swing to the ball, NEVER needs to travel anywhere but UNDER THE FOAM! The problem is that the swing path leading from behind your head directly to the ball is a path that travels to the right of the target line.

Yes, the key to the proper swing path is that it travels OUT to the ball. And that path to the right is one that slicers loathe. They hate it so much that they re-direct their energy to the left as quickly as possible during the downswing, which throws the club to the outside of the foam, obviously a recipe for disaster.

I'm going to backtrack a bit and cover this concept in greater detail. The club head's journey from the top of the backswing down to impact is typically referred to as the swing path. To eliminate the slice, it is imperative that your club travels on a path UNDER the imaginary foam board en route to the ball.

The good news is, the previous keys have prepared you to do just that! The result will be pure contact and a glorious draw.

To help visualize a good swing path that results in a draw, imagine a tennis serve or even bowling. In both cases, energy moving to the right creates spin to the left!

Now that we know where we're sending the club head, let's hit the ball!

Swing Key #3

Impact

It is now the MOMENT OF TRUTH. Yes, we are actually going to make contact with the ball!

Everything we've done so far has a very clear purpose: to help you achieve a reliable, powerful, and non-slicing position at the moment of impact. That would be very different from a typical slicer's impact position, where their left shoulder spins frantically to the left as they lurch into impact.

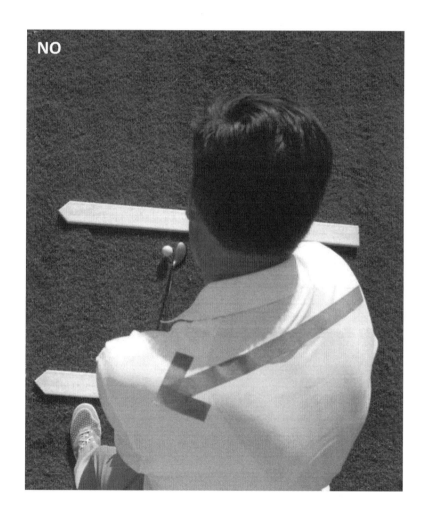

Slice-Free Golf helps you achieve a position where your shoulders will actually feel closed at impact, which mirrors the Upper Body Alignment described in Get Set Key #3.

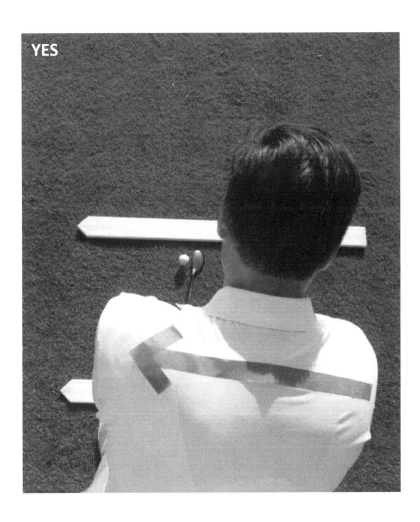

A great way to get the feel for this critical impact position is to imagine you have an eye directly in the center of your chest.

If you're a slicer, that eye will most likely be looking AHEAD of the ball at impact

In the *Slice-Free Golf* swing you need to achieve the positions shown where the imaginary eye is looking slightly BEHIND the ball at impact.

It is also very helpful to have the *actual* eyes in your head, *and* your face, focusing on a spot just behind the ball.

To further emphasize the importance of this key, here are sequential positions of the downswing and impact of a typical slicer.

And the same positions of the proper *Slice-Free Golf* draw swing.

Steps One and Two put you into a perfect draw position at impact. It takes some patience and practice, but the pay-off is INCREDIBLE!

And all of this leads smoothly to Step Three.

Step Three

•

Release

Release Key #1

Let It Happen

The feel, the look, and most importantly, the comfortable power of a great release have been sought by golfers all around the planet. Ironically, the beautiful position shown on the opposite page is merely the result of successfully completing Steps One and Two. It just HAPPENS!

As mentioned in Get Set Key #5, consistent grip pressure and relaxed wrists are important components of the release. If this seems like a contradiction, consider what you have to do to snap someone with a towel. Your wrists and your arms need to be supple enough to create speed, yet your grip on the towel needs to be firm enough to keep it from slipping out of your fingers. Or think about old-fashioned mercury thermometers. They needed to be cleared with a similar flip of the wrist. Do that with stiff, tight wrists? Impossible. Not gripped firmly enough? There's a thermometer shattered on the floor.

Mimicking these two motions will help you to understand the subtleties of the golf grip. Go ahead—grab a towel, twirl it into a rat tail, and snap someone in the butt. If they object, just explain that you're working on your golf game.

A typical slicer will generally create energy that moves outside the target line before cutting dramatically across the ball to the left. This disgusting action usually involves a very anxious left elbow, which tends to hurry past the ball and to the left well before the club strikes the ball.

The result is a club head firing to the left with a slightly open clubface

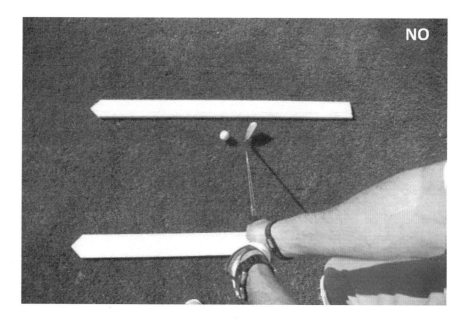

and wide separation between the elbows.

Actually, slicers have so much energy moving left prior to impact that they are programmed NOT to release. If they did, the contact would feel great, but the ball would end up waaaay left of the target! With all that energy cutting to the left, the slicer is actually wise NOT to release. Slicers develop what appears to be more of a hold than a release. Together, the leftward path and holding the clubface open create sidespin that hopefully fades or slices the ball back into play. Unfortunately, the ball limps weakly back into the short grass and distance suffers tremendously.

Keep in mind that the ugly photos of a poor release on the opposite page depict slicers who have yet to master *Slice-Free Golf*. For you, my trusting reader, the days of a swing that looks like that are LONG GONE! If you've been following the keys and working with the drills you will find later in this book, your swing will have a more natural and powerful motion.

Relax, trust the sequence of *Slice-Free Golf* steps, and the release JUST HAPPENS!

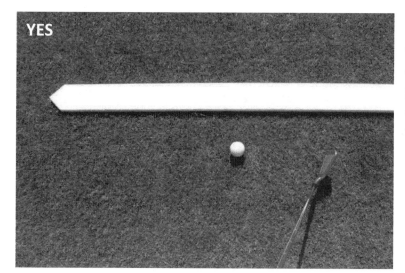

This is what you will see as your club head travels inside the target line (under the foam) then hits the ball square to the line

And what your release will look like when you LET IT HAPPEN. Supple wrists and a swing under the foam lead directly to the position shown on the right.

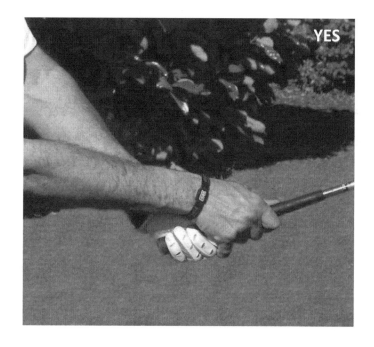

Congratulations, release has been achieved!

Now, let's finish the swing.

Release Key #2

A Balanced Finish

There are many styles and different looks even among the very best golf swings, but there are certain common denominators among the world's best golfers. Finishing with balance is something you will see in every great, repetitive swing. While it is true that success with the keys so far will likely lead naturally to a balanced finish, I am NOT going to assume that Release Key #2 is guaranteed.

If your swing leads to an off-balance finish, then you have a swing that is bound to be inconsistent. Conversely, a balanced finish is a sign of efficiency and evidence of an effective, repetitive motion. If balance is always achieved, your swing is becoming more consistent and reliable!

As I've said, there are different swing styles that lead to different finish positions, but great swings lead to a finish that can be held (or posed) without fighting gravity or feeling unstable. The general look? It will vary, but a stable front leg, a released right foot (resting on the toe), and a chest and belt buckle facing the target (or even left of it depending on your flexibility).

From a down-the-line perspective, you'll notice there is still a hint of spine angle, the sole of the trailing foot is totally exposed and the knees are fairly close together as the finish pose is held.

To test your balance, hold your finish until the ball you've struck actually hits the ground. You may feel a bit silly holding the pose for this length of time, but this is a great habit to develop. Working on this (especially as you practice) WILL make you a better player.

When you're not on the course, interlock your fingers in a pretend grip and watch your finish in the mirror. If you're really confident, try the drill with your eyes closed—a real test of balance! Practice achieving a balanced finish whenever possible. Do it as you warm up, between shots on the range, with each practice swing, or even without a club.

Congratulations!

At this point I want to officially pronounce you a *Slice-Free Golf* graduate!

You are no longer the short ball hitter in your group. You are no longer weak. You no longer fear a dog-leg left. You no longer need to choose a 5-iron at a par-3 where your buddies just hit 8-irons. No, times have changed. You now possess the ability to produce a relaxed, powerful and repetitive draw.

And golf is about to become much more enjoyable!

Step Four
Practice, Practice, Practice

Step Four? What the heck??? This is supposed to be a three-step program!

But what kind of PGA Professional would I be if I didn't encourage my students to practice? *Slice-Free Golf* works (you know that by now)—and it works EVERY time. If you want to keep it working, though, you need to practice.

It will take some time to get truly comfortable with the new key positions you have so diligently achieved. A *Slice-Free Golf* swing you can trust comes with repetition and a very close watch on Steps One through Three, which is why Step Four is simply PRACTICE, PRACTICE, PRACTICE! And I don't just mean to go to the range and blindly flail through bucket after bucket of balls. Just as you learned to swing effectively, you need to learn to practice effectively, too!

Take *Slice-Free Golf* with you. Page 79 is a duplicate of page 78. This is not a printing error. The idea is for you to cut this page neatly out of the book and take it with you whenever you plan to visit the range or the golf course. Fold it up and put it in your golf bag. Make copies of it and wallpaper your living room. Put a copy on the nightstand next to your bed, put one in each bathroom, under your pillow, etc. Go through the proper *Slice-Free Golf* key images in your mind whenever possible.

You'll also find many drills at www.slicefreegolf.com that you can print and take to the range. The site has a continually-updated set of training tools, swing tips, and other information you'll find useful.

We've already covered numerous drills you can use at the range (and elsewhere) to ingrain *Slice-Free Golf* into your mind and body. The following section includes several bonus drills you can use for the same purpose. I encourage you to start every practice session with a few of these exercises, then work them into your routine until the moves become second nature.

With proper *Slice-Free Golf* practice, you will succeed in all situations:

1. Alone on the driving range
2. Alone on the golf course
3. With friends or associates on the golf course
4. In competition on the golf course
5. In competition with a significant amount of your money on the line

As this list points out, the first signs of massive *Slice-Free Golf* improvement will quickly show on the driving range. And before long, you will transfer your new swing to any pressure-packed situation this game can throw at you!

Visual Guide To *Slice-Free Golf*

Align Base

Centered Turn

Ball Position

Under Foam

Align Upper Body

Impact

Square Clubface

Let Release Happen

Your Grip

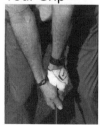

Balanced Finish

Cut Out Visual Guide To *Slice-Free Golf*

Align Base

Ball Position

Align Upper Body

Square Clubface

Your Grip

Centered Turn

Under Foam

Impact

Let Release Happen

Balanced Finish

Don't Slip!

•

Bonus Drills

Slice-Free Golf
Drill #1

Pigeon Toe

Pigeon Toe helps to keep your hips—and even your shoulders—from spinning left too quickly during the downswing. Start by settling in to your new *Slice-Free Golf* address, then turn your left toe inward (to the right).

This awkward-feeling position will actually lead to an effective release of the club while slowing down your hip and body rotation. This drill also assists with keeping your chest from pointing ahead of the ball prior to impact.

Try this with some small practice swings at first, then tee up a ball as you increase the length of your swing to three-quarters or so. Hitting balls with this drill is sure to better-synchronize your impact positions, and quickly lead to the sweet feel of a powerful draw. Pigeon Toe will lead you to more birdies!

Slice-Free Golf
Drill #2

Fromunda The Grip

The grip is a personal and very critical component of *Slice-Free Golf*. Remember the specifics of the proper left hand position, then use this drill as you apply your right hand to the club.

To get a better feel for where your right hand should be, bring it to the grip *from under* (fromunda) the handle.

By approaching the grip from this lower location, your right hand is far more likely to assume an effective slice-free position.

Great, smooth rotation of the clubface will be the result as long as you don't grip too tightly. Enjoy the power of the draw!

Slice-Free Golf
Drill #3

Spaghetti Arms

Another way to check your address position is to turn your arms into spaghetti. Dump that low-carb diet of yours for a few minutes; this is a rare occasion where spaghetti (or at least the image of it) is actually helpful.

Assume your *Slice-Free Golf* set-up. Without losing your posture, let your arms hang. They won't hang straight—there will likely be a gentle bend—but be sure to let all the tension out of your arms so they feel like strands of wet spaghetti. If your setup was correct, your arms should have a comfortable space between your hands and thighs.

If you were in a slicer's stance, the space between your left hand and thigh is much smaller than the space created on the right side. You may also notice that from a slice set-up, you now have a clear look at your left toe, while your right hand obstructs the view of your right toe.

The arm hang from a square set-up will create equal space between your hands and thighs on both sides.

To achieve a *Slice-Free Golf* set-up that is extra-effective, adjust your posture so that your right hand hangs a touch closer to your body than your left (opposite of the typical slicer set-up).

Slice-Free Golf
Drill #4

One Leg Is Better Than Two

All other components of your new *Slice-Free Golf* address position are exactly as described in the book, but with this drill, you no longer have two legs.

Literally put your feet together and take some small half swings. If you sway or lunge or lean, you'll fall! If you don't believe me, duct-tape your legs together and try doing this drill the wrong way—it will NOT be pretty.

This is a great drill to help you stay centered. You will also feel how the club swings *around* you. With the one-leg drill, the club will approach the ball on the proper path (from the inside) and the release will happen quite naturally.

Start with small, relaxed practice swings and slowly work your way up to a three-quarter swing. But be sure to keep your balance!

This is a drill you can use while actually hitting balls, so go ahead and tee up a ball directly in the center of your stance and take a relaxed, centered swing. Relax, keep your axis steady and find a nice rhythm. You may actually want to tee up several balls in advance, so you are better able to build a nice smooth tempo.

Slice-Free Golf
Drill #5

The Foot Wedge

No, this is not the famous foot wedge Judge Smails used to shamelessly improve his lie in *Caddy Shack*! (Please take an hour and a half and watch the best golf movie ever made. By the way, hatred for slicing is highlighted in the film!). This *Slice-Free Golf*-approved foot wedge drill would also be illegal if you were to use it on the course during an official round, but it is an excellent way to encourage a more centered swing on the practice range.

As mentioned earlier, many slicers tend to sway back and away from the target during the backswing. This drill can help put a stop to that and help you achieve a centered, rotational backswing.

Simply place a rolled-up golf towel under the outside of your right foot as you step into your new SFG address. The towel will help to prevent you from rolling your weight to the outside of that foot during your backswing.

As you take the club to the top, you should now feel the sensation of staying centered as well as a feeling of proper hip rotation, NOT hip sway.

As you swing to the finish, your weight will naturally move to your left leg and your right foot will leave the towel.

Go ahead and actually hit some balls as you perform this drill. It will definitely help you appreciate the full, centered turn!

Slice-Free Golf
Drill #6

The Shadow Knows

If you're eligible for the Super Senior division of your club championship, you may remember that the title of this drill was a line from a popular radio program from 1930 to 1954. While the Shadow was known as the most effective crime-fighter of his time, there is another shadow that is equally as effective when it comes to improving your golf swing—yours.

Place two balls on the ground, and while taking your Slice-Free Golf address, position the shadow of your head between the golf balls.

When you watch the world's best players, notice how their heads stay relatively still from address until impact. While a certain amount of movement is acceptable, anything excessive leads to severe inconsistency. The Shadow drill allows you to actually swing a club as you practice maintaining a stable, centered position.

Make a smooth, full backswing and pause near the top to take note of your shadow's position.

Then swing down slowly and pose in the impact position, watching to see that your shadow is still in place. Note that if you were to continue on to the finish, your head would not stay in place—it would naturally move out of the markers.

If your shadow did not touch either ball from address to impact, then you are familiar with the sensation of keeping your head relatively still. But if you see a lot of movement, keep practicing this drill. Better ball-striking and sweet draws are just around the corner. The shadow knows....

Slice-Free Golf
Drill #7

Off The Wall

By now you may think I'm a bit off the wall, but trust me, when it comes to slice elimination, I am totally lucid.

Off the Wall is very similar to another drill that is widely used to help people feel a centered turn. Making an imaginary swing while maintaining contact between your forehead and a wall (until just after impact) is a classic drill and it certainly has some merit. The drill discourages excessive side-to-side and rising and lowering of the head, but there is another plane to consider.

My Off the Wall drill addresses another common mid-swing movement—straight forward (toward the ball). Many golfers unknowingly move their head toward the ball during the backswing. This movement can lead to poor balance, an outside—in (or over-the-foam) swing path, and perhaps worst of all, hosel contact (also known as a "sh*nk"—I don't even want to spell it!). Unfortunately, it's very difficult for a golfer to feel this form of excessive movement—unless you use this drill.

With the standard head-touching-the-wall drill, a player will not know if they have a tendency to move toward the ball. Since there is already contact with the wall, any movement forward is hidden. The subtle increase in pressure on the player's forehead will probably not be noticed. But the Off the Wall drill is the perfect way to address this issue. Move forward, and you will feel your forehead touch the wall.

Take your proper *Slice-Free Golf* address position and imagine you have a club in your hands (do not actually use a club). Set up in front of a wall so that your forehead is approximately one inch away from the surface.

From this position, take a comfortable backswing. If your head moves forward significantly , you will bump the wall. That is NOT what you want to feel!

Keep rehearsing until you can make comfortable practice swings without touching the wall. It won't be long before you are turning and swinging better (and you can say goodbye to the sh*nks)!

Slice-Free Golf
Drill #8

Mirror Line

One of the best tools for individual practice is a simple full-length mirror—indoors or out.

Using masking tape (and a carpenter's level if you want to be exact) apply a level horizontal line to the mirror. That line should run across the very top of your head as you view your reflection from the address position. Smaller vertical lines of tape can be applied to frame each side of your head.

Much like the Shadow drill, start at address and move to the top of your backswing, while checking that your head maintains its position.

Then swing down and pose at the impact position, while watching the mirror to make sure that your head stays fairly centered

Remember this drill focuses on your position from address to impact only. Don't try to stay inside the lines if you continue past impact to a balanced finish.

Slice-Free Golf
Drill #9

Scrape The Siding

Most slicers have heard of the term over the top, or my version, over the foam. Many of my favorite drills in this book are designed to reverse that problem and keep readers UNDER the foam, and able to attack the ball from inside the target line. The ScrapeThe Siding drill provides a clever way to assure an inside-out approach to impact.

First, find an appropriate wall, preferably outside. Holding a mid-iron, assume your proper *Slice-Free Golf* address position with your back to the wall. After carefully taking your club to the top of the backswing, shuffle back until the club-head touches the wall.

At this point you should be in mid-swing posture with your heels parallel to the wall. The next move is critical!

From this top position, the typical slicer gets very anxious with the shoulders, and throws the club outside the target line (or over the foam).

Rather than hurling the club outward, you should relax your arms, and allow them and the club to drop a bit as you begin your downswing. Keep the club head in contact with the wall as you begin to rotate your hips toward impact.

Sliding the club head along the wall for a foot or so will force your arms and shoulders to be more patient during the downswing. Practice this motion of scraping the wall, and your slice will disappear in a hurry. It's well worth the cost of some touch-up paint!

**Slice-Free Golf
Drill #10**

Three Pockets

Keeping your spine angle consistent from address until impact helps to keep your club head on the right path (approaching the ball from under the foam or from the inside). Unfortunately, it is very common to see slicers in a far more vertical position at impact than they had at the start of their swing.

Changing the spine angle to such a degree can lead to a very poor energy path. Luckily, I have a perfect drill for this malady. The Three Pocket drill can be done on the range with the help of a chair.

Take your new *Slice-Free Golf* stance, then shuffle backwards until your back pockets gently contact the chair.

As you move to the top of the backswing, your hips will rotate so that only your back right pocket touches the chair.

As you begin the downswing, your hips will unwind and both pockets will touch.

Remember, it is essential that they KEEP rotating so that only your left back pocket will be touching the chair at impact!

As you continue through the ball, you will actually finish in balance with the side of your front left pocket contacting the chair. Don't worry if you can't get all the way to that position. Levels of flexibility vary greatly from player to player.

The Three Pocket drill will help you to maintain a powerful spine angle, but remember to incorporate the *Slice-Free Golf* keys as you practice. It's easy to maintain contact with the chair, but maintaining contact as you properly make a full, centered turn may be a bit more challenging. Keep practicing, and a more compact and powerful sensation will develop. By the way, using a chair allows you to actually hit balls while doing this drill, so feel free to tee one up once you get a good feel for this motion.

The Three Pocket drill can also be done without a club in the comfort of your own home. Mimic your grip, assume your *Slice-Free Golf* stance, gently back up against a wall and achieve the positions I've outlined. But DON'T USE A CLUB in your home or you're likely to do some serious damage!

Slice-Free Golf
Drill #11

Uphill Battle

For those who slice, golf can certainly feel like an uphill battle. Ironically, that same hill can help to eliminate the shameful banana ball! Most slicers have a downswing that travels outside, then down and across the ball in a steep, chopping motion. The Uphill Battle drill is a quick way to find a shallower approach to the ball. And the drill isn't really a battle— it's actually quite easy!

Find a hill or a slope that elevates the ball at least a few inches above your feet. From your *Slice-Free Golf* address position, take a few practice swings and feel how the elevated ground requires your swing to be flatter or more around your body. This flatter or shallower path into the ball is ideal for a powerful draw swing. Feel the club head rotate naturally as you take what will feel more like a baseball swing around a stable center.

If possible, hit some balls from this position. Enjoy the draw, and realize how easy it is to swing under the foam when the ball is above your feet. Keep that same feeling as you head back to the level teeing ground!

If you don't have a slope to use (or just want to impress your friends), you can really exaggerate that same flat swing feeling by dropping to your knees and swinging at the ball.

Want another exaggerated move to help feel that shallow path? Stick an old shaft into the ground then tee up a ball on it and swing away.

You'll either WOW your friends or snap two shafts!

Slice-Free Golf
Drill #12

Cold Shoulder

This is one of my favorites because you can do it on the range or just about anywhere including during an actual round of golf. The Cold Shoulder is an excellent way to synchronize your upper body with the rest of a powerful new draw swing.

Take your *Slice-Free Golf* address position, then extend your left arm straight out in front of you and place your left hand on the grip of a vertically positioned long iron, hybrid or fairway wood.

In your right hand, grip a shorter iron or wedge, and gently make some very relaxed half swings.

The left shoulder of most slicers will spin dramatically left early in the downswing, creating a swing path that goes outside the target line and across the ball to the left. This drill forces that left shoulder to be more patient.

When you perform this exercise correctly, the imaginary eye in the chest demonstrated earlier in the book will look at or behind the spot where the ball would be as you swing into the impact zone. And you will have an accurate sensation of swinging under the foam.

This is NOT a full-swing drill! Stay centered, relaxed, and let the club swing freely with small swings. The Cold Shoulder is very effective when trying to achieve proper upper-body positioning at impact.

Many of my students create this same feeling without the help of a guide club. They simply make some mini swings under an extended left arm.

Slice-Free Golf
Drill #13

Bottle Ball

This drill is brilliantly simple and very effective. Tee up a ball just inside of a standing plastic water bottle (for obvious reasons, NEVER use a glass bottle!).

Utilizing your _Slice-Free Golf_ keys, comfortably address the ball. Then, slide your club out a bit further and address the bottle.

From this unique position, the idea is to take a normal backswing but take extra care to keep your downswing further to the inside than normal. If you successfully resist the temptation to swing over the foam and keep your club moving from the inside, you can successfully strike the ball, NOT THE BOTTLE, with your clubface.

The slight re-routing of the club required to avoid the bottle and hit the ball is the OPPOSITE of the typical slicer's path. This drill hones the proper inside-out path required for a beautiful draw!

And here's a huge bonus tip:

Thanks to tee markers, you actually have 18 CHANCES TO CHEAT (legally!). Teeing up the ball as shown allows you to get the benefit of a guide for each tee shot during your round!

Trust me, when you address the ball this way when you're on the course, the tee marker certainly helps you keep the club moving from the inside on the downswing. But be careful. If you choose to tee up close to a marker, and swing on a slicer's path, the results could be embarrassing—and potentially harmful!

109

Slice-Free Golf
Drill #14

Under Tube And Over Tube

I love this drill! Yes, it may require a trip to your local hardware store, but believe me, it's well worth the trip!

The first step is to lay down some alignment aids (or clubs) to create your work station. Then find two old shafts (without club-heads attached) or two wooden dowels and push them both into the ground, at an angle that closely resembles the angle of your chosen practice club at address. The shaft to your right should enter the ground just outside the target line, and the shaft to your left (the target side) should be inside the target line. At the hardware store you can find some pipe insulators or go to a variety store and look for some tube-style pool floats like we did. Apply these foam tubes to each of the guide shafts (or dowels) as shown, for greater visual effect as well as protection from the unlikely possibility of striking one of the guides with your club.

After taking your proper *Slice-Free Golf* stance, start with some slow practice swings, being careful to swing under (or *inside*) the tube to your right...

then over (or *outside*) the tube to your left.

Missing the tubes properly on both sides will begin to groove a proper inside-out path. After some smooth (and centered) practice swings, tee up a ball in the appropriate spot in your station. Keep that beautiful, rhythmic practice swing path, miss the tubes on both sides, and watch your ball draw!

112

Slice-Free Golf
Drill #15

Show Me The Ball

This drill helps you feel the forearm rotation of a successful release. With a golf ball enclosed in your left fist, position that hand in a pre-impact pose. While slowly moving that hand to a post-impact position, rotate your left forearm so that the ball will balance in your left palm as you open your fist.

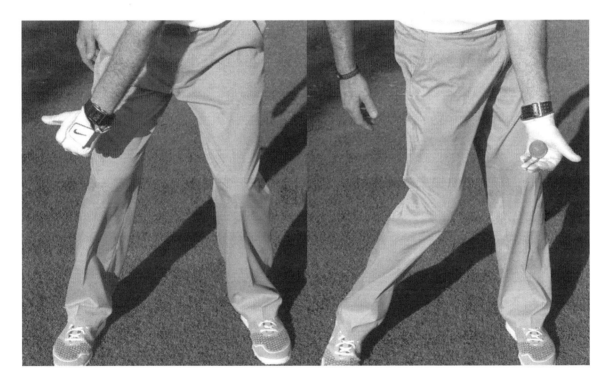

Seems simple, right? Well it is! But that doesn't mean this is an exercise to take lightly. Keep doing it, and really concentrate on the natural rotation taking place. In order to do this drill effectively, your left elbow does NOT drive toward the target. It actually stays relatively close to your side. Be sure to note that left elbow position as you complete a few more reps. It is a critical component of this very effective drill!

Slice-Free Golf
Drill #16

Head Cover Deodorant

Just because you slice doesn't mean you literally stink, but Head Cover Deodorant is an exercise that will sure make your golf game smell a lot sweeter! To be specific, this drill will help the slice-inclined to properly release the club through the impact zone.

Position a head cover up into your left armpit (thus, my deodorant reference) and pinch it into place with your upper arm.

From a proper *Slice-Free Golf* address position, take some relaxed half swings and be sure to *not* let the head cover drop.

You should feel some upper body rotation, and keeping the head-cover in place will encourage the club to release properly through impact instead of being held open.

This drill leads to natural forearm rotation, and beautiful extension through impact.

Remember, Head Cover Deodorant is designed for smaller swings. If you take a full swing the cover will drop as you near completion of either the backswing or the finish.

Slice-Free Golf
Drill #17

See The Light

In the dark about your swing path? Try this drill to "see the light" and begin to enjoy the effortless power of solid contact that comes from swinging the club on the proper path. First, you'll need a light source. There are expensive laser devices on the market, but a simple cylindrical flashlight will do the trick. Set up an alignment station and create an extension of the target line.

Turn on the flashlight, grip it as if it were a club and take your proper address position, pointing the beam at a spot on the target line where the ball would lie. Next, reverse the flashlight so the beam is shining on your midsection.

Now, take a mini backswing keeping your left arm parallel to the ground. Take note of where the beam is pointing. If the path of your backswing is on-plane and you've made a comfortable wrist hinge, the beam should be pointing at a spot on the target line. Too steep, and the beam will be inside the line. Too flat and the beam will be outside the line.

Complete your backswing, but as you head back down toward impact, freeze once your left arm gets back to parallel.

Is the beam on the line again? If so, the club is still on plane.

Relax and continue to swing through impact. When your right arm is parallel to the ground after impact, the flashlight beam will again point at the target line in front of where the ball was. This is proof that your swing is continuing to the finish on-plane.

Practice the See the Light drill and you will begin to repeat the sensation of a very efficient, banana-free swing!

Slice-Free Golf
Drill #18

Hip Check

Many slicers have a pronounced figure 8 shape to their swing path. They generally start their backswing on a very inside track because they know that inside-out is a good path to encourage, but then things go awry.

At the top of their backswing, slice fears kick in. In that fraction of a second before the downswing begins, the slicer's mind envisions a huge, ugly banana ball. That disgusting image causes the slicer to re-route their downswing in an effort to prevent the ball from launching to the right. The inside backswing morphs into an outside (or over-the-foam) downswing that will start the ball left of target but end up producing a hideous slice. Such re-routing actually causes the club to follow a very detrimental figure eight path.

The Hip Check drill literally reverses that path and turns it into one that will produce a powerful draw.

Set up a station defined by parallel guides and place a tee in the ground where the ball should be. Approximately 18 inches behind that tee (and slightly inside of the target line) place a head cover or a water bottle.

After assuming your new *Slice-Free Golf* address position, begin your take-away, being careful to keep the club-head *outside* of the bottle as shown.

After reaching the top of your backswing, begin the downswing with the understanding that the club-head will swing back to the tee on a path to the *inside* of the bottle—an exaggerated version of the proper *Slice-Free Golf* path.

This outside-the-bottle take-away and inside-the-bottle downswing REVERSES the slicer figure eight and creates an exaggerated power-draw figure eight!

Why do I call this drill the Hip Check? When you begin the downswing correctly, your right elbow will move toward (and can even make contact with) the right hip as you approach impact on a path from inside the bottle.

Practice this reverse figure eight and take notice of your right elbow position during the downswing. Make sure it's close to that right hip before reaching impact. After a while, put a ball on the tee and see the results. Be sure to maintain proper *Slice-Free Golf* positions as you practice!

Slice-Free Golf
Drill #19

Elbow Room

You've seen the look of a natural and proper release several times in this book. If your club head is on the proper path and your body and forearms rotate in a natural and comfortable fashion, you'll notice that your elbows are fairly close together following impact .

With the slicer, the elbows are often too far apart through impact, which prohibits a natural and effective release.

If there is excessive space between your elbows prior to, during, or just after impact, this Elbow Room drill is perfect for you! There are specific training aids made for this drill, but you can get the same effect with a partially-deflated volleyball or a spongy kickball.

Assume your new *Slice-Free Golf* address, and note the space between your elbows. Securely position the ball in the gap.

Then, take some small relaxed swings, taking care to keep the ball in place.

This drill should only be done with small half swings or less and you should be sure to stay centered, turn properly, and utilize your normal wrist-hinge and forearm rotation. You can even tee up a ball and try some little chips and pitches with this motion.

Elbow Room will help you to maintain the correct distance between your elbows through the critical impact zone. If those elbows spread, the ball will drop...and you need to keep working!

Slice-Free Golf
Drill #20

Play Miss Tee For Me

I'm a Clint Eastwood fan—isn't everybody? Do you remember that great movie he made, *Play Misty For Me*? This version of Play Miss-Tee is one of the simplest of the *Slice-Free Golf* drills and perhaps the most effective.

As always, start with your new *Slice-Free Golf* address position. Utilize a couple of guides to run parallel with your target line. Tee up a ball to the inside of the far guide and then place two additional tees in the ground as shown.

Then remove the ball and tee from the center, and take some practice swings that allow the club head to pass through the remaining two tees without touching them.

If you're interested, try searching the internet for James Douglas Edgar, who was probably the first golf instructor to utilize this incredible drill. His invention, the gate, helped golfers in the hickory shaft era to cure their slices.

This drill encourages the essential inside-out path—a perfect path that leads to a beautiful, powerful draw. Now re-tee that ball in the center and repeat the path of your practice swings. Pure contact with a gentle draw is sure to follow. Clint would be proud of you!

Slice-Free Golf
Drill #21

Fit To Be Tied

Another way to keep your elbows under control—and your club head on the proper path—is to tie them together for a few practice swings. This drill forces you to turn effectively and requires a comfortable wrist hinge and release as you do so.

You can use just about any sort of elastic band that's long enough to stretch across your upper arms (we used a girl's headband!)

After taking your proper address position, stretch the band around your forearms as shown and re-grip the club.

Using proper *Slice-Free Golf* keys, take a few small swings with the band in place. Limit the drill to half swings, but feel free to tee up some balls and make some little pitch shots. With your elbows pinned, you'll get the sensation of a very synchronized and connected movement.

If you really want to ingrain a "connected" swing, have a buddy wrap a bungee cord completely around your upper arms and body. The wrap should pass over your biceps (above the elbow) and totally circle your torso. I've also used rope, a belt, even duct tape. It's a bit severe, but it works!

Just make sure your buddy is still around to untie you when your practice session is over!

**Slice-Free Golf
Drill #22**

Toe First

For a little extra help in the rotation department, the Toe First drill is just the ticket!

Set up a hitting station, then find an impact bag (or an old pillow case or even a duffel bag filled with towels or laundry). You'll also need an extra shaft or dowel and a length of foam pipe insulation or a tubular pool float. Insert the extra shaft just inside the target-line guide to your right, and apply the foam insulator. This foam-covered shaft should match your shaft angle at address and act as a guide for your backswing and downswing.

Place the laundry bag just past where the ball would be (with something behind it, perhaps even a wall, to keep it in place).

Now, settle in to your *Slice-Free Golf* address position. Take a half swing back over the tube-covered shaft.

Then swing back down under it through the point where the ball would be and gently strike the bag. Half speed is all you need for this exercise.

The key is that the TOE of your clubface needs to strike the bag first! In order to do this drill properly, you will need to rotate the clubface through impact (in an exaggerated fashion) to strike the bag Toe First.

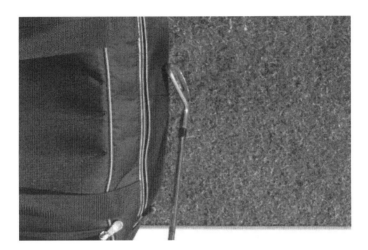

Over the tube, under the tube, toe in the bag. Over the tube, under the tube, toe in the bag. Yes, the motion is rather exaggerated, but this drill is designed to promote forearm and clubface rotation and believe me, it works!

After a few minutes of practice, tee up a ball on the range and make that same relaxed swing. Visualize going over the tube on the backswing, under the tube on the downswing, and contacting the bag with the club's toe first. That ball will zip away with a piercing little draw!

Slice-Free Golf
Drill #23

The Boxer

When you slice, golf can feel like a fight. Ironically, boxing can assist with adjusting your swing. But unlike a true pugilist, you won't need fists and a mouth guard.

An empty cardboard box can help you "K.O." that banana ball! The Boxer drill points out the two most critical aspects of curing a slice: the position of the clubface at impact, and the path that your clubface is traveling on through impact.

First, set up in your alignment station with a mid-iron and a proper address position. Instead of a ball, place a long, empty cardboard box parallel to your alignment aids. One end of the box should be even with the point where your club would first contact the ball at impact. The other end will be further forward and pointing directly down the target line.

Address the back edge of the box, take your club to the top of the backswing, and prepare for the important portion of this drill.

In super slow motion begin your downswing, being careful to deliver your club head from inside the target line (under the foam). Pause before contact with the box and be sure that you are meeting the cardboard squarely. You certainly would not want to touch the box with the heel of your clubface first.

After meeting the box squarely with the leading edge of your club, slowly move the club ten or twelve inches further through impact. This little motion has MAJOR implications. A slicer will tend to move the impact side of the box quickly to the left, causing the far end to swing to the right.

To eliminate the slice and groove the powerful path of a draw, reposition the box and try again. Meet the end of the box squarely, then slowly rotate your body (and the clubface) as you continue on a slightly inside-out path through the impact zone. The near end of the box will move slightly right, and the far end will swing to the left a bit.

This exaggerated move will help you eliminate the slice. It is also a helpful image to visualize as you make actual swings on the range.

Slice-Free Golf
Drill #24

Thumbs Up

This is another great mirror drill.

Face the mirror and begin your backswing. At the point where your left arm is parallel to the ground, look into the mirror to take note of two key positions. The first is a long left arm, the other is the back of your left hand—with your thumbs pointing up to the sky.

Although they appear to be straight up, your thumbs will actually be pointing on a slight angle that matches the plane on which your club is moving.

Then swing through impact so that your right arm is parallel to the ground on the target side. Check in the mirror again to be sure you are now looking at the back of your right hand and a long right arm. Your thumbs will again be pointing up in correspondence with the swing plane. A perfect example of a successful release!

The beauty of mirror drills is that you can mimic a grip and actually practice inside without a club whenever you'd like—day or night, in the rain, sleet, or snow. NO EXCUSES! Just be sure to achieve the *Slice-Free Golf* positions as you practice.

Slice-Free Golf
Drill #25

Slap Shot

It's no accident that many hockey players are pretty good golfers. A hockey stick shares many key design components of the golf club and the relationship of player-to-puck is similar to that of golfer-to-ball. Additionally, the slap shot or even the flip pass in hockey features a release that slicers would envy. Slap Shot is a very appropriate title for this drill, which will train you to feel the forearm rotation and release of a Wayne Gretzky scoring shot—and experience a beautiful draw!

First, take your new *Slice-Free Golf* address position, then slide your right hand down beyond the grip to the shaft of the club. Keep the club above the ground as you take a few small practice swings. This split-grip will exaggerate the rotation of your forearms, and the clubface will close rapidly through the impact area.

Don't hit balls with this drill, but enjoy the feeling of a dramatic release motion. Keep this sensation as you return to a normal grip, and watch that ball draw!

Just remember, golf is a gentleman's game...no high-sticking or cross-checking!

Slice-Free Golf
Drill #26

A Little Help From A Friend

When you create a proper path and swing from the inside, your ball will launch slightly to the right and draw back toward the target. The Help From A Friend drill encourages a beautiful draw in a highly memorable way.

It does require some preparation. Don't spend too much time on the details, but find a piece of cardboard or foam-core (life-size would be awesome but not necessary) and cut out a human silhouette. Then find a picture of a good friend or one of your golfing buddies, and enlarge the face of your subject on a copy machine to a size that corresponds to the size of the silhouette. Affix it to the cardboard and tape a shaft or a couple dowels to the back so it will stand up.

Now, position your "friend" so that he faces you and stands three or four paces closer to the target and just a couple feet left of the target line. The idea is simple: Trust and perform the *Slice-Free Golf* system, or lose your "friend."

After setting up this very memorable practice station, the goal of the exercise is obvious. If you follow the *Slice-Free Golf* steps properly, the ball you strike will launch to the right of your new assistant and draw back around him to the target line. Stray from the program, and your cardboard buddy is *toast.* It's easy to see why this drill is a fan favorite at the range!

Yes, this is a bit morbid, but don't take it too seriously—have some fun!

Instead of the likeness of a friend or golfing buddy, I used to recommend using the student's mother-in-law or boss, but the cardboard cut-out used to get destroyed much quicker. This should go without a mention, but please, never use an *actual* friend for this drill! We had some fun with Photoshop to produce our illustration.

The silhouette makes this drill very memorable, but hitting around a shaft stuck in the ground can create the same sensation.

More

●

Slice-Free Golf

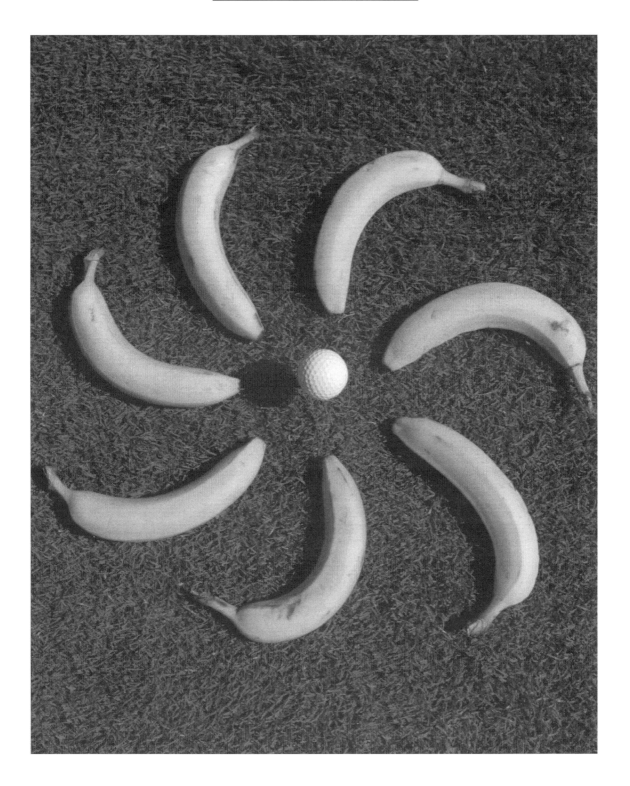

More Ways To Beat The Slice

By now you know that with the right information in the proper sequence the dreaded slice can be truly eliminated. But it does require diligence. Making a lasting change calls for commitment and dedication—and it never hurts to get a little additional help.

The Keys and Drills featured in the three steps to *Slice-Free Golf* have been tested and proven throughout my 20 years as a golf instructor. They have been carefully assembled to provide any struggling banana hitter with a simple program to cure the slice. The program works! And if you've read the preceding pages, you know the joy of pure contact and possess the power of a draw.

But there's MORE.

My goal was to produce the ultimate, most comprehensive resource for banana ball elimination. These additional topics will give you even more ways to explore and ENJOY the powerful world of *Slice-Free Golf*!

Fitness & Nutrition

Do you need to be in peak physical condition to play great golf? No. But improving your level of fitness can do wonders for your game—and for your life in general. There are golf-specific workout programs that you can investigate, but regardless of the routine, success will require dedication. One other note: while *Slice Free Golf* does provide the remedy for slices, I am not a doctor. You should consult with an actual physician before starting any fitness program.

While strength is certainly helpful, golf is not the NFL so you don't need to freak out with barbells and protein shakes. The key to golf fitness is to strengthen the core muscle groups for stability while increasing your range of motion for speed. A proper fitness regimen will improve your performance and also help protect you from injury. Incidentally, golf provides an easy option for those who are looking for a little extra exercise—walking the course! A simple way to get in better shape is to pass on the golf cart and use your legs.

Even if you do not commit to a specific training plan, you should still allow time to warm up before stepping on the first tee. It is far too common for golfers to race to the course, run from the car to the first tee, fumble frantically through their bag looking for a glove and a ball, then expect to enjoy a "relaxing" round of golf. Instead, force yourself to arrive at the course 30 minutes early and take the time to stretch and loosen up on the range. Take plenty of relaxed practice swings, then start with some three-quarter shots. The goal is NOT to see if you can empty an entire bucket of balls in a half hour. The warm-up gives you time to release some tension, loosen your muscles and focus your thoughts for the upcoming round. Arriving early allows a golfer to prepare both physically and mentally. A little less panic can produce a great deal more success.

Your body, now a *Slice-Free Golf* machine, needs fuel, too, and you should try to put good stuff in the tank. Filling it with the wrong fuel can lead to a lack of energy and loss of focus. That doesn't mean you can't treat yourself to a doughnut here and there, but if you're like most golfers, it wouldn't hurt to put a little more thought into your diet. In some cases, visiting a certified nutritionist would be a good move, but many of us just need to make a commitment to eat better and possibly adjust our meal schedule.

If you're like me, enjoying a big lunch or a heavy breakfast just before a round of golf is not the way to go. In fact, stopping after the ninth hole and cramming a cheeseburger into my mouth is also trouble. I seem to play best when I've had a light meal before play, then supplement with small, healthy snacks periodically throughout the round. This technique seems to keep energy levels balanced, and it also eliminates the disruption of stopping in the middle of my round to sit and choke down a turkey club.

It is also very important, especially in warmer climates, to drink plenty of water before, during and after play. Staying hydrated is important, and here's a great point to remember: If you wait until you're thirsty, it's too late.

Since I'm on a wellness rant, I'll give one more piece of advice. Protect yourself from the sun. I know a ton of people who wish they took better care of themselves in this regard. Wear a hat, apply the sunblock (the higher the SPF rating, the better the protection) and even consider wearing shades between shots. The better you care for your body, the longer you can enjoy *Slice-Free Golf*!

Continual Improvement
With A PGA Professional

Golf is a sport that is FUN and can be enjoyed by people of all shapes, ages, and levels of experience. Frankly, I *cringe* every time I hear someone say that golf is difficult. It's NOT, especially when you have a copy of *Slice-Free Golf* in your hand! In fact, the biggest challenge instructors may face is helping students find attainable goals within an acceptable time frame. *Unreasonable* expectations—regardless of the player's ability level—will inevitably lead to frustration.

The key is to develop a fair plan of action like the clear roadmap laid out in this book. *Slice-Free Golf* will quickly lead struggling slicers to a sweet new world of power and consistency. But periodically checking in with a PGA professional will also help keep you on track.

A quick note on locating a PGA pro. Get referrals, ask around, talk to and even interview potential instructors, and don't commit to a series of lessons until you've found the right instructor FOR YOU. Once you've clicked with a particular PGA pro, it is helpful to stay with him or her for a while. You're likely to improve at a faster rate with a clear plan and a consistent message and style. A different instructor for every lesson can sometimes lead to confusion.

Refer to *Slice-Free Golf* often, and implement the specific drills that address your biggest anti-slice challenges. And if you need an extra set of eyes to keep you on track, look me up on-line at www.slicefreegolf.com or be sure to contact a local PGA professional.

What's In Your Bag?

Set make-up can be a very personal topic, and quite frankly, the perfect combination can vary quite a bit from one player to the next. Only 15 years ago, it was common to have a driver, three wood, five wood, two-through-nine irons, pitching wedge, sand wedge, and putter as a 14 club set. But with today's technology and the introduction of the hybrid clubs, things have changed quite a bit.

I think most players would benefit from higher-lofted fairway woods in general, and greater attention should be paid to the scoring clubs for shots inside 110 yards. Pay attention to the distances your clubs produce. Any wide gaps should be investigated, especially with your wedges. While there is no substitute for a personal club-fitting and distance session with a PGA Pro, if I were asked to put together a set of clubs that best suits the majority of golfers, it would look like this:

Driver

Fairway wood (15-18 degrees)

Hybrid (18-21 degrees)

Hybrid (22-26 degrees)

4 – 9 irons

PW (48 degrees)

54 degree wedge (with 10 – 14 degrees of bounce)

58 degree wedge (with 8 – 12 degrees of bounce)

Putter

Consult with your local PGA Professional for personal specs and greater detail.

Club Fitting, Ball Fitting & Getting A Grip

The fastest way to *Slice-Free Golf* is to carefully read this book. But investing in the proper equipment can have a significant impact on the shape and quality of your shots, too. Does that mean that you can actually buy your way to a better game? Well, in many cases, yes!

First of all, let's take a look in your golf bag. If you notice the words "mashie" or "niblick" on any clubs, it's time to step into the current century. Same holds true for any other club a termite might find appetizing. I want to make sure that none of my readers are struggling with persimmon or laminated woods.

But even if you have relatively new technology, that doesn't mean you have the right clubs for your swing. The best plan of action is to see your local PGA professional and get an assessment of your current equipment. A certified club fitter will only need a few minutes to determine if your sticks suit you.

Keep in mind there are differing goals when it comes to fitting clubs. Here's an analogy: If your waist size is 42, and you've just committed to a weight loss program, you probably don't want to head to the mall and spend a thousand dollars on size 42 pants. You might want to hold off until you see how the diet is progressing. There's a similar challenge in club-fitting. With a golfer who is unlikely to change his or her posture or swing plane, a fitter has no issue. They'll match the clubs to that player's swing. But with a golfer who intends to adjust posture, and work on improving swing path and positions, a club-fitter needs to have a little "room for improvement" built into the assessment.

Which is why the PGA professional is the best option. The pro will have an open discussion with you, assess a reasonable set-up / swing improvement plan (if you plan to make a change) and lead you to the clubs that will assist with your improvement. Although irons remain traditional in terms of fitting, we are now in the age of adjustable drivers and fairway woods, which does give the consumer many options. But just because you can change the loft and/or face angle of a driver doesn't mean you've got the right shaft or grip.

Speaking of grips, do not underestimate their importance! Grips that are slick or worn from age can actually lead to hand and arm tension. When grips lose their tackiness, a player needs to apply more pressure to keep the club in position, which can lead to inconsistency and a poor release. Believe me, when it comes to tension, too tight = too far right (banana city). New grips (and a new glove) will help you relax while still maintaining control of the club. When you drop off your clubs to have them re-gripped, I strongly recommend choosing a new set from the Lamkin line. The Lamkin Co. has been in business for more than 85 years, their quality is unmatched, and they have an exciting product line.

Another piece of equipment that needs to be addressed is your golf ball. Not enough attention is given to choosing the ball that best suits your swing. There are golf balls that are designed to minimize the effects of sidespin and can truly make your missed shots more playable. If you have a slower swing speed, there are golf balls that are easier to compress which will help to deliver maximum distance. In short, it is well worth the effort to use the right ball for your swing.

As you can tell, there are many details in the world of golf equipment. My advice: see your local PGA pro, openly discuss what your golf plans and expectations are, then spend some time having your clubs and grips assessed and even determine the best ball for your swing. The proper equipment can make a huge difference, and assist you with a *Slice-Free* game.

Mind Games

Anyone who has ever played this game knows that golf involves a significant psychological component. *Slice-Free Golf* is a specific program with proven results. It gives a slicer a step-by-step guide to success—but the program is designed for completion at the range. In order for a player to take this exciting new swing to the course, there must be trust, confidence, and a simple plan. This book (along with diligent practice and repetition) will produce those three ingredients and lead to dramatic improvement on the course.

A player who can stay relaxed and focused during a round is a player who is certain to succeed. Miles of text have been written on the mental side of golf, and believe me, it would be easy to babble on for another 30 or 40 pages. But instead, I will try to simplify the subject.

The practice range is the place to focus on swing changes and work on improvement. The actual golf course is a place to play the game. Does that mean you should forget everything you're working on when you tee it up on the links? NO. But the best golf is played when you're relaxed and swinging freely. And it's impossible to truly relax when you've got a laundry list of 20 different swing thoughts bouncing around in your skull as you address the ball.

The solution?

Before going to the course, decide on just one pre-swing / set-up thought, and only one actual swing thought that you've been working on. Then consider this simple, on-course routine: After selecting your club, make a focused practice swing that achieves both of your chosen thoughts, and form a clear mental picture of the upcoming shot— including a successful result. Then address the ball, take one last glance at your target, and do your best to relax and repeat the sensation of your practice swing.

Committing to this routine will help you to focus clearly on limited objectives, visualize success, and stay more relaxed. Don't fret if the results don't match your visualization. Stay the course, resist the temptation to change your key thoughts, and continue to utilize the routine before each shot. This technique will keep you "in the present," help you to tune-out distractions, and allow you to enjoy your round and appreciate the environment between shots.

When you're able to simplify your process, focus on a routine, and relax, you will succeed in taking *Slice-Free Golf* to the course.

The Laws of Ball Flight

How many initial directions can a golf ball take after being struck in the standard manner by the face of the club? I'm sure some of you are thinking that the possibilities are endless. Believe it or not, the answer is three.

Initial Launch Directions

1. Straight down the target line
2. To the left of the target line
3. To the right of the target line

Once the ball begins its journey in one of these three directions, sidespin or a relative lack thereof will then promote one of three shot shapes.

Shot Shapes

1. Remain relatively straight on its initial path
2. Curve to the left of its initial path or
3. Curve to the right of its initial path

Three initial launch directions multiplied by three potential shot shapes equals nine possible flight paths—known as the Nine Laws of Ball Flight.

The primary cause of the initial launch direction is the position of the club face relative to the target line.

The primary cause of the spin, or the shape of the shot, is the path of the club head, or the direction of energy prior to and through impact.

Swing Paths

1. From too far inside to the right (will break thru foam after impact)
2. From inside to square (all under the foam)
3. From above or outside to the left (will break thru foam before impact)

Why do you need to know this? Aside from impressing your friends, this knowledge may help you diagnose your own swing problems if you can't get to your PGA professional right away. Watch your ball to see if it matches one of the nine possible ball flights on the following pages.

The white rectangle represents the angle of the club face. The white arrow is the path of the club head as it approaches impact and the gray arrow is the resulting ball flight.

Pull Draw / Hook

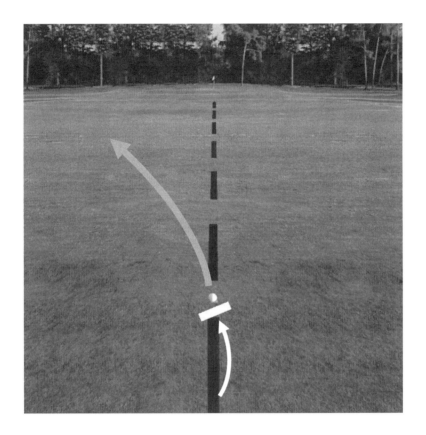

Swing path is a touch left
Club face closed

Straight Pull

Swing path is left
Club face square to swing path

Pull Fade / Slice

Swing path is too far left
Club face open relative to swing path

Square Draw

Swing path a touch right
Club face square

Straight Square

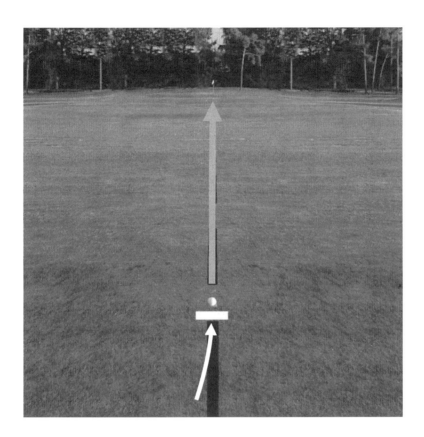

Swing path square
Club face square

Square Fade

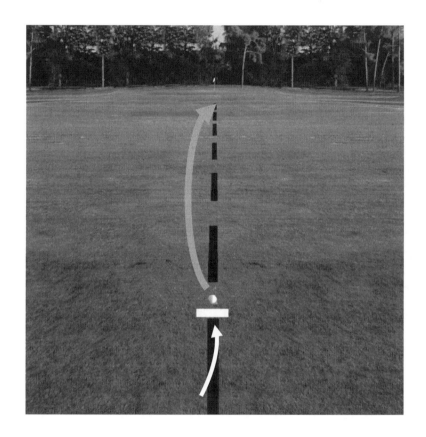

Swing path a touch left
Club face square

Push Draw / Hook

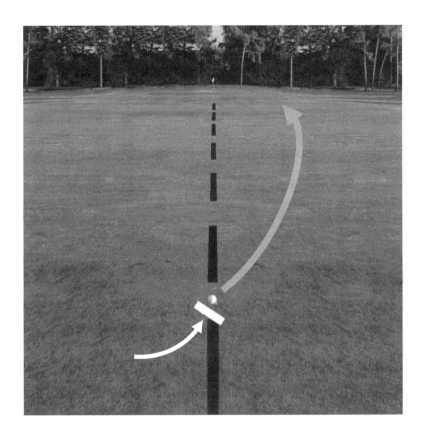

Swing path is too far right
Club face closed relative to swing path

Straight Push / Block

Swing path right
Club face square to swing path

Push Fade / Slice

Swing path is a touch right
Club face open

Ball flight produced by *Slice-Free Golf*

About The Author

Brian Crowell is the PGA Head Golf Professional at GlenArbor Golf Club in Bedford, NY, and has been a golf instructor since 1991. In addition to his many golf professional duties, Brian is also a television broadcaster, radio host, and author.

Brian has been featured as the co-host of NBC-TV's *Golf Digest Equipment Special* in 2009, 2010, and 2011 along with Dottie Pepper. These nationally televised programs aired on Sundays in March, highlighting the very latest in golf industry innovations. In 2011, Brian joined CBS as a broadcaster at The Masters. He was the play-by-play announcer teamed with Bobby Clampett on *Masters In-Depth*, which aired on Direct TV, Masters.com, and cbssports.com. As a member of the NBCSports.com broadcast team since 2007, Brian has covered many major golf tournaments including the U.S. Open (Men's, Women's, and Senior), U.S. Amateur (Men's and Women's), The President's Cup, and The Ryder Cup. He was featured nationally on the USA Network as a commentator for the PGA Tour's Chrysler Classic of Greensboro, and has been an analyst / interviewer for MSG network. Brian has worked alongside Bill Patrick, Jennifer Mills, Jimmy Roberts, Judy Rankin, John Cook, Billy Ray Brown, and Phil Blackmar, among others.

Radio listeners hear Brian on his live weekly sports radio program, *The Clubhouse*, throughout the golf season on AM 1230 WFAS in New York. Brian has interviewed numerous celebrities, professional athletes and dignitaries on this popular show. Brian has also been a frequent guest instructor on AM 1050 ESPN and has been a featured guest on Peter Kessler's *Making the Turn* (Sirius 209 and XM 146) as well as several other radio shows in the metropolitan New York area.

Brian's work as a writer has been featured in a number of books, newspapers, and major magazines. His weekly column in New York Metro has gathered great reviews, and he was a contributing author in Donald Trump's book, *The Greatest Golf Advice I Ever Received*. In 2007, Brian released his first book, *Teach Yourself Visually, Golf* with Wiley Publishing, followed by *Visual Quick Tips, Golf*, released in 2008. Brian's work can also be seen in *The Secret of Golf* by George Peper and *Golf Rx* by Dr. Vijay Vad. He has appeared in many major golf magazines, been a contributing writer for *GOLF* magazine, and recently wrote a four-page instructional article in the *Met Golfer* magazine.

Brian has an extensive record of service to the Metropolitan Section of the PGA and was appointed to the position of Secretary after holding other executive and board positions in recent years. Brian has also won several awards, including the Horton Smith Award for Outstanding Contributions to Education. In 2011, he was appointed to the National Public Relations Committee of the PGA of America and was given a position on the Advisory Board for the Lamkin Grip Company. As a highly regarded instructor in the Metropolitan Section and beyond, he has given countless golf lessons, clinics, and demonstrations. In 2003, Brian was named one of America's Best Instructors by National Consumer's Research, and in 2005 was selected as one of the Top 50 Junior Golf Instructors in the country by US Kids Golf.

He has been a featured spokesman on-line and in infomercials, and Brian recently co-produced and starred in the golf instructional DVD, *Get in the Game*. He was also instrumental in launching the website GolfersMD.com, and is currently a member of their advisory board, the host for their video content, and one of the site's featured experts. Brian was also seen in three national network television commercials for Smith and Wollensky Steakhouses with co-star Craig Stadler. In addition to various assignments as an emcee and a featured speaker, he has been a consultant and a model for a number of successful projects, including the recently released *Quamut Guide to Golf.*

Brian's many interests include all other sports, outdoor activities, automobiles, and music. He even performs as the bassist / tenor sax player for Faze2, a rock band. As a proud father and husband, Brian loves to spend time with his wife Wendy and their three incredible children Kevin, Casey, and Christina.

Acknowledgements

Completing a project like *Slice-Free Golf* requires time, effort, and some serious assistance. Seeing the finished product is gratifying, but I certainly won't forget the help and inspiration I received throughout the process. First, I would like to thank my friend Dave Donelson on several counts…editing, photography, layout, design of www.slicefreegolf.com, and marketing advice.

A very special thank you to the legendary Gary Player for his motivation and support and for writing the foreword for *Slice Free Golf*. Dottie Pepper, Scott McCarron, Rob Labritz, Debbie Doniger, Shawn Humphries, Carl Alexander, John Zanzarella, Frank Male, Jr., Billy Ray Brown, Joe Messa, and Dr. John Viscovitch were all instrumental in providing me with incredible endorsements.

Also I want to thank John Lee, PGA, his staff, and everyone at the beautiful Imperial Country Club in Naples, FL for providing an excellent photo shoot venue. I also appreciate the warm hospitality and perfect accommodations provided by Michael Oliveri.

A number of my close friends and supporters have had a hand in my success to this point and deserve my thanks:

The owners, members and fellow staff members of GlenArbor Golf Club
Steve Herz and Jeff Feldman of IF Management
The PGA of America
PGA Magazine
Nike Golf and representatives Mark Vassalotti and Kathy Colwell for their many years of support
TaylorMade/Adidas Golf and Reva Freshman and Dan Reinhardt for their support in years to come
NBC Sports, Tommy Roy, and Jon Miller
CBS Sports, Lance Barrow, Kenny Mack, Harold Bryant, Steve Karasik, Ryan Galvin, and Andy Goldberg
The Lamkin Grip Company
Golf Digest and Bob Carney
John Zanzarella of Zanzarella Sports Marketing
Mark Jeffers of MarSar Production
Paul Radetsky, Will Fenn, Pete and Rich Shea
Jim O'Mara and Jim Dwyer
Alex Mairone and Hammock Beach Resort

I apologize to anyone who may have temporarily slipped my mind, there are so many who have been so helpful to me.

Of course, the biggest "thank yous" are reserved for family. Bill and MaryLou Bahr, Lynne and Jeff Diener, Addison and Eleanor Crowell, Lloyd and Lena Kniffin, and my ultimate role models, Stewart and Carolyn Crowell. Finally and most of all, thank you to my wife, Wendy, and our three incredible kids, Kevin, Casey and Christina.

Forgive me if you feel like you're at the Oscars—but that felt good.

A Couple More Things...

The most successful golfers are those having the most fun. I hope you enjoyed Slice-Free Golf, and if you were previously a slicer, that you will now find more enjoyment on the course!

As fun as it was to write this book, I get even more enjoyment making personal appearances and speaking directly to audiences of all sizes. Whether sharing my keys for a Slice-Free life, unveiling winning secrets to business golf or just providing a comfortable introduction to the sport, I truly love the opportunity to entertain.

"Each time Brian has addressed the PGA members of the Metropolitan Section, he has provided a very entertaining experience! With effortless presentation skills, Brian makes it easy to focus on the content of his messages and keeps the audience engaged. He is forward-thinking, and always delivers topics that are relevant to our profession."
-- **Carl Alexander**, Chairman, Metropolitan PGA Education Committee

"Brian Crowell is a talented and dynamic young man. He is an excellent and entertaining communicator and teacher. His in-person presentation captivates the audience and the audience absorbs what he has to say. And, that's what a great teacher does."
-- **John Zanzarella**, President, Zanzarella Sports Marketing

"We have had many celebrities over the years but Brian captivated the audience like no other. His simple approach to the swing with the "big eye" visual was put in play immediately by many players. It works! His passion for the game and life was evident during his speech at the banquet. A phenomenal addition to our event."
-- **Frank Male, Jr.**, Tournament Chairman, FR Male Sr Memorial Golf Classic

"Brian has the gift of making everyone in attendance feel as if he is speaking directly to each person in his audience. His tips on *Slice-Free Golf* were simple to understand and, in my case, quite easy to implement. Thank you, Brian!"
-- **Joseph Messa**, President, Bridge Metal Industries, LLC

"Brian displays unbridled enthusiasm while teaching golf. More importantly, whether you're a beginner or an advanced player, he has a way of passing along knowledge in a very simple and concise manner. He clearly loves his job!"
-- **Dr. John Viscovich**

For more information, contact me at brian@slicefreegolf.com.

Life can be stressful...golf should be fun!

The Ultimate *Slice-Free Golf* Website

To keep your game slice-free, visit www.slicefreegolf.com. The website provides a ton of additional slice-eliminating content. You will find video tips, expert swing advice, news and notes, photos, and reader participation opportunities as well as training aids, nutrition and fitness, and important information from our great sponsors.

Of course, there's also an easy way to order more copies of *Slice-Free Golf*. If your group would be interested in customized editions or bulk pricing, please let us know.

To contact me or find out more about my personal appearances, please check out www.slicefreegolf.com.

Made in the USA
San Bernardino, CA
23 May 2014